30 Instant Hangover Cures

To Get Rid of The Morning After
Nightmare - The Only Cookbook You
Will Ever Need

BY

Daniel Humphreys

D1360184

License Notes

No part of this Book can be reproduced in any form or by any means including print, electronic, scanning or photocopying unless prior permission is granted by the author.

All ideas, suggestions and guidelines mentioned here are written for informative purposes. While the author has taken every possible step to ensure accuracy, all readers are advised to follow information at their own risk. The author cannot be held responsible for personal and/or commercial damages in case of misinterpreting and misunderstanding any part of this Book

Table of Contents

Introduction

Greetings readers! Thank you so much for purchasing my book! I really hope you find a great go to recipe to immediately get rid of that monstrous hangover. If you are hung-over right now, you probably don't want to do any reading, and I don't blame you! Trust me, I know the feeling, having killer hangovers is the reason why I wrote this book. Anyway, if you are sober, here is some helpful information to get you through a night out without feeling like you are on deaths door the next morning.

- Line your stomach before you go out, in other words, eat something
- Drink loads of water while you are drinking and before you go to bed at night
- Drink in moderation – don't keep knocking back shots
- Drink white instead of brown spirits
- Drink some alcohol the next day

Here are 30 simple recipes to beat any hangover!

1: Orange and Sugar Mix

A simple mixture of orange juice, sugar and salt

(Preparation time: 5 minutes)

Ingredients

- 1 teaspoon of salt
- 5 cups of distilled water
- 8 teaspoons of sugar
- ½ a cup of orange juice

Directions

1. Combine the Ingredients in a large bowl and mix together thoroughly.

2. Pour into a bottle screw the lid on tight and shake vigorously.

3. Drink slowly throughout the day.

4. Store in a cool place and don't keep for more than 24 hours.

2: Ginger, Tangerine and Sugar

A powerful mixture of ginger, tangerine and sugar.

(Preparation time: 5 minutes)

Ingredients

- 1 piece of ginger, 1 inch in size, peeled and chopped
- 3 teaspoons of sugar
- 3 teaspoons of tangerine extract
- Boiled water

Directions

1. Boil a saucepan of water.

2. Put the ginger, sugar and tangerine extract into a tea cup.

3. Pour the boiling water over the top and allow it to steep for 15 minutes.

4. Sip slowly.

3: Ginger Tea

You will be surprised at what a simple cup of tea can do to a hangover.

(Preparation time: 20 minutes/Servings: as many cups as you like)

Ingredients

- Ginger tea bags
- Boiling water
- Sugar (optional)

Directions

1. Boil water in a saucepan.

2. Put the tea bag and sugar into a tea cup.

3. Pour the boiling water over the top and allow it to steep for 15 minutes.

4. Sip slowly.

4: Peppermint Tea

Let the soothing taste of peppermint heal your body.

(Preparation time: 20 minutes/Servings: as many cups as you like)

Ingredients

- Peppermint tea bags
- Boiling water
- Sugar (optional)

Directions

1. Boil water in a saucepan.

2. Put the tea bag and sugar into a tea cup.

3. Pour the boiling water over the top and allow it to steep for 15 minutes.

4. Sip slowly.

5: Asparagus

It has been scientifically proven that asparagus protects the liver against damage from alcohol and alleviates hangover symptoms

(Preparation time: 13 minutes Serves: 4-5 servings)

Ingredients

- ½ a pound of fresh asparagus
- ½ a teaspoon of salt
- ½ a teaspoon of fresh ground black pepper
- 3 cloves of minced garlic
- 3 tablespoons of Parmesan cheese

- Cooking spray (olive oil)

Directions

1. Preheat the oven to 200 degrees C.

2. Line a baking tray with cooking foil.

3. Wash the asparagus and trim the ends off.

4. Arrange the asparagus onto the baking tray.

5. Spray the asparagus with the cooking spray.

6. Sprinkle with salt, pepper, garlic and Parmesan cheese.

7. Massage the Ingredients into the asparagus with your hands.

8. Spray the asparagus again with the cooking spray.

9. Bake for 8 minutes.

10. Remove from the oven and eat.

6: Resurrection Smoothie

This smoothie will raise you back to life.

(Preparation time: 5 minutes/Serves: 2 servings)

Ingredients

- 6 peeled oranges
- 1 cup of mixed frozen berries
- 1 banana, ripe
- 2 tablespoons of yogurt
- 1 tablespoon of honey
- A pinch of salt
- Fresh blueberries to garnish
- Honeycomb to garnish

Directions

1. Combine all Ingredients apart from the fresh blueberries and the honeycomb in food processor. Blend the Ingredients until smooth.

2. Pour into a glass, garnish with honeycomb and fresh blueberries and drink.

7: Hangover Juice

A tasty juice that will knock that hangover right out.

(Preparation time: 10 minutes/Serves: 1 serving)

Ingredients

- 2 carrots
- 2 oranges
- 1 beetroot
- 2 celery sticks
- 1 lemon
- 1 piece of ginger, 1 inch

Directions

1. Wash the Ingredients thoroughly.

2. Peel the lemon, beet and orange.

3. Put the Ingredients into the juicer and juice according to the manufacturer's instructions.

4. Pour into a glass and drink.

8: Hangover Cure

It definitely will cure your hangover.

(Preparation time: 5 minutes/Serves: 1 serving)

Ingredients

- 1 cup of chopped cantaloupe
- 3 cups of spinach
- ¾ cup of red grapes
- 2 sticks of celery

Directions

1. Put all Ingredients into a juicer and juice according to the manufactures instructions.

2. Pour into a glass and drink.

9: Poached Eggs for a Hangover

Tasty and soothing at the same time, what more can you ask for.

(Preparation time: 10 minutes/Serves: 1 serving)

Ingredients

- 2 eggs
- 1/3 cup of catsup
- 1/3 cup of water
- 1 tablespoon of vinegar
- 1 tablespoon of butter
- 1/3 cup of cheddar cheese
- 2 slices of toast

Directions

1. Put the water, vinegar and catsup into a frying pan and stir to combine. Put a tight fitting lid onto the frying pan and heat over a medium temperature until it starts to bubble.

2. Add the butter and let it melt and then stir it in.

3. Break the eggs on top, put the lid on the frying pan and allow the **Ingredients** to simmer for 3 minutes.

4. Use a slotted spatula to remove the eggs and arrange onto the toast.

5. Pour the sauce on top of the eggs, top with cheese and eat.

10: Creamy Mushrooms on Toast

Oh, so delicious, your hangover won't stand a chance.

(Preparation time: 10 minutes/Serves: 1 serving)

Ingredients

- 1 slice of wholemeal toast
- 1 ½ tablespoons of light cream cheese
- 1 teaspoon of rapeseed oil
- 3 handfuls of chopped mushrooms
- 2 tablespoons of skimmed milk
- ¼ teaspoon of wholegrain mustard
- 1 tablespoon of snipped chives
- 150 ml of freshly squeezed orange juice

Directions

1. Spread a knifefull of cheese onto the toast.

2. Heat the oil in a frying pan and cook the mushrooms.

3. Add the milk, the mustard and the rest of the cheese. Stir to combine.

4. Spoon onto the toast and top with the chives.

5. Eat with a glass of orange juice.

11: Hangover Berry Omelette

Fruits combined with eggs, delicious!

(Preparation time: 7 minutes/Serves: 1 serving)

Ingredients

- 1 large egg
- 1 tablespoon of skimmed milk
- ¼ teaspoon of cinnamon
- ½ a teaspoon of rapeseed oil
- 100 grams of cottage cheese
- 175 grams of chopped raspberries, blueberries and strawberries

Ingredients

1. Whisk the egg in a small bowl, add the cinnamon and the milk and continue to whisk.

2. Heat the oil in a frying pan over medium heat and cook the egg until both sides are golden brown.

3. Move the omelette onto a plate, spread the cheese over the top, sprinkle the berries over the top, fold in half and serve.

12: Baked Eggs and Salmon

Eggs and fish will definitely do the trick.

(Preparation time: 15 minutes: Serves: 6 servings)

Ingredients

- 6 white rolls, crusty
- 25 grams of melted butter
- 6 slices of smoked salmon
- 6 medium eggs
- Some snipped chives

Directions

1. Heat the oven to 200 degrees C.

2. Slice the top off each roll and scoop the bread from the inside.

3. Arrange the rolls on a baking tray and brush the insides of each roll with the butter.

4. Place a slice of salmon inside all pieces of bread.

5. Crack an egg on top of the salmon.

6. Bake for 15 minutes.

7. Sprinkle the chives over the top and serve.

13: Blueberry and Apple Bircher

A simple delicious recipe that will destroy your hangover.

(Preparation time: 10 minutes/Serves: 4 servings)

Ingredients

- 200 grams of porridge oats
- ½ a teaspoon of ground cinnamon
- 500 ml of apple juice
- 4 grated apples
- 200 grams of blueberries

Directions

1. In a large bowl, combine the porridge oats, grated apples, apple juice, cinnamon and blueberries. Stir to combine and let it stand for 5 minutes before eating.

14: Bacon and Garlic Butties

You won't be able to eat just one of these!

(Preparation time: 25 minutes/Serves: 6 servings)

Ingredients

- 6 slices of rindless bacon
- 1 loaf of bread
- Butter
- 3 tablespoons of tomato chutney
- 1 large clove of garlic, peeled and sliced in half

Directions

1. Preheat the grill to 200 degrees C.

2. Heat the frying pan over a medium temperature and cook the bacon for until it becomes crispy and golden.

3. Slice 6 thick pieces of bread and butter them.

4. Spread the chutney onto 3 slices of the bread.

5. Top with 2 slices of bacon.

6. Top with the rest of the bread and press down well.

7. Grill the butties until golden brown.

8. Remove the butties from the grill and move both sides with the garlic and serve.

15: Berries and Banana with Cinnamon Porridge

Nothing but good old spicy porridge to beat a hangover.

(Preparation time: 20 minutes/Serves: 4 servings)

Ingredients

- 100 grams of porridge oats
- ½ a teaspoon of cinnamon
- Cinnamon for serving
- 4 teaspoons of Demerara sugar
- 450 ml of milk, skimmed
- 3 sliced bananas
- 1 punnet of strawberries, slice the tops off and cut them in half
- 150 grams of natural yogurt, fat free

Directions

1. Combine the oats, half of the bananas, milk, sugar and ½ a teaspoon of cinnamon. Stir to combine and then bring to a boil on high heat.

2. Reduce the temperature down to low and cook for 5 minutes.

3. Divide into 4 bowls, top with strawberries, yogurt the rest of the banana and a dash of cinnamon and serve.

16: Orange and Chicken Salad

A Simple but heavenly recipe.

(Preparation time: 25 minutes/Serves: 2 servings)

Ingredients

- 1 packet of green beans, trimmed
- 1 large avocado
- 100 grams of chopped watercress
- 1 fennel bulb
- 2 oranges
- 2 tablespoons of olive oil
- 2 shredded cooked chicken breasts

Directions

1. Boil some salted water in a medium saucepan and cook the beans for 5 minutes.

2. Drain and rinse under cold water.

3. Transfer the beans into a bowl.

4. Slice the fennel bulb finely and cut away the core.

5. Peel the avocado, slice it and add it to the bowl.

6. Add the olive oil and toss to combine.

7. Scatter the chicken over the top and serve.

17: Banana and Peanut Butter on Toast

Quick and easy to make, full of hangover boosting nutrients.

(Preparation time: 10 minutes/Serves: 1 serving)

Ingredients

- 2 slices of granary bread
- 1 medium banana
- ½ a teaspoon of cinnamon
- 1 tablespoon of crunchy peanut butter

Directions

1. Toast the bread.

2. Slice the banana, put it on one slice of the toast and dust with cinnamon.

3. Spread the other slice of toast with peanut butter.

4. Put the two pieces of bread together, cut into triangles and eat.

18: Jeeves Concoction

This quick concoction will get you back to normal in no time.

(Preparation time: 5 minutes/Serves: 1 serving)

Ingredients

- 1 raw egg
- ¼ ounce of Worcestershire sauce
- ¼ ounce of Tabasco

Directions

1. Crack the egg into a glass.

2. Add the Worcestershire sauce and the Tabasco.

3. Stir together thoroughly.

4. Consume in one gulp.

19: The Red Mary

There's nothing like more alcohol to get you back on your feet.

(Preparation time: 5 minutes/Serves: 1 serving)

Ingredients

- 1 ounce of vodka
- ½ a cup of tomato juice
- A pinch of ground black pepper
- 1 splash of Tabasco sauce
- 3 splashes of Worcestershire sauce
- 1/8 teaspoon of pure horseradish
- A splash of lime juice
- Black olives for garnish

Directions

1. Pour all Ingredients into a tall glass and mix together thoroughly.

2. Drink in one sitting.

20: The Red Eye

You won't have red eyes after this drink.

(Preparation time: 5 minutes/Serves: 1 serving)

Ingredients

- 12 ounces of beer
- 4 ounces of tomato juice
- 1 egg
- 1 ounce of vodka

Directions

1. Pour the tomato juice into a glass.

2. Pour the beer over the top.

3. Crack the egg over the top.

4. Drink in one gulp.

21: The Distressed Bastard

You won't feel distressed after this.

(Preparation time: 5 minutes/Serves: 1 serving)

Ingredients

- 1 part of gin
- 1 part of bourbon
- 3 parts of ginger ale
- 1 dash of bitters
- Ice

Directions

1. Put the ice in the cup and pour the rest of the Ingredients over the top.

2. Stir to combine.

3. Garnish with lime and drink.

22: The Breakfast Bartender Hangover Cure

And it will certainly cure your hangover!

(Preparation time: 5 minutes/Serves: 1 serving)

Ingredients

- 2 ounces of vodka
- A pinch of ground coriander
- 1 basil leaf
- 1 handful of cherry tomatoes
- A pinch of celery salt
- A pinch of pepper
- A pinch of chopped chives
- Ice

Directions

1. Add all of the Ingredients to a food processor and blend until smooth.

2. Then pour into a glass and drink.

23: Cinnamon Toast

Delicious cinnamon toast.

(Preparation time: 10 minutes/Serves: 1 serving)

Ingredients

- 2 slices of raisin cinnamon bread
- 2 tablespoons of unsalted softened butter
- 1 tablespoon of sugar and extra for sprinkling
- ½ a teaspoon of ground cinnamon

Directions

1. In a small bowl, combine the cinnamon, sugar and butter and stir to combine.

2. Toast the bread.

3. Spread the cinnamon mixture over the toast.

4. Dust with sugar and eat.

24: Banana Pancakes

Pancakes are good, but even better with bananas

(Preparation time: 20 minutes/Serves: 4 servings)

Ingredients

- 1 ¾ cups of all purpose flour
- ¼ teaspoon of salt
- 2 large eggs
- 2 teaspoons of baking powder
- 1 tablespoon of sugar
- 1 ¼ cups of whole milk
- 4 tablespoons of melted unsalted butter

- 2 sliced ripe bananas

Directions

1. In a large bowl, combine all of the dry Ingredients and stir together thoroughly.

2. In another large bowl, combine the wet Ingredients and whisk together thoroughly.

3. Combine the wet and the dry Ingredients and stir to combine.

4. Add the bananas and stir to combine.

5. Heat a small frying pan over medium heat.

6. Pour the batter into the frying pan and cook for 2 minutes on both sides or until the pancakes becomes golden brown in color.

7. Repeat until the batter is finished and serve.

25: Sausage and Sweet Potato Hash

This recipe is so delicious, you will be begging for more.

(Preparation time: 45 minutes/Serves: 6 servings)

Ingredients

- 2 tablespoons of unsalted butter
- 1 thinly sliced medium onion
- 4 cloves of minced garlic
- 1 pound of Italian sausage, casing removed and crumbled
- 4 large sweet potatoes

- 2 tablespoons of olive oil

Directions

1. Preheat the oven to 200 degrees C.

2. Heat the butter in a medium frying pan over a medium temperature.

3. Add the garlic and onions and cook for 6 minutes.

4. Heat another medium frying pan over a medium temperature.

5. Cook the sausage for 10 minutes and then drain the fat.

6. Peel the sweet potatoes and slice them into ½ inch cubes. Put them into a bowl; add the olive oil and salt and pepper. Toss to combine.

7. Pour the sausage and the onions into the potatoes and stir to combine.

8. Pour the potato mixture onto a baking tray and bake for 30 minutes.

9. Remove from the oven and serve.

26: Bacon Maple Pancakes

Delicious pancakes make with bacon and maple.

(Preparation time: 35 minutes/Serves: 6 servings)

Ingredients

- 12 slices of bacon
- ½ a cup of maple syrup and extra for serving
- 2 large eggs
- 1 ¼ cups of whole milk
- 4 tablespoons of melted butter
- ¼ teaspoon of salt
- 1 ¾ cups of all purpose flour

- 2 teaspoons of baking powder
- 1 tablespoon of sugar

Directions

1. Heat a large frying pan over a medium temperature.

2. Cook the bacon until it becomes crispy.

3. In a large bowl, combine all of the dry Ingredients and stir together thoroughly.

4. In another large bowl, combine the wet Ingredients and whisk together thoroughly.

5. Combine the wet and the dry Ingredients and stir to combine.

6. Crumble the bacon and add to the batter.

7. Heat a small frying pan over medium heat.

8. Pour the batter into the frying pan and cook for 2 minutes on both sides or until the pancakes becomes golden brown in color.

9. Repeat until the batter is finished and serve.

27: Hash Corned Beef Recipe

Everyone loves moms home cooked corned beef.

(Preparation time: 50 minutes/Serves: 4 servings)

Ingredients

- 2 tablespoons of unsalted butter
- 1 finely chopped yellow onion
- 1 ½ cups of finely diced corned beef
- 3 cups of diced cooked potatoes
- 4 large eggs

Directions

1. In a medium frying pan, melt the butter over medium temperature.

2. Add the onion and cook for 7 minutes.

3. Add the potatoes and corned beef and stir to combine.

4. Use a spatula the press the mixture down into the frying pan.

5. Reduce the heat to low and then cook for another 15 minutes until it turns golden brown in color.

6. Flip over and cook for another 5 minutes.

7. Divide the corned beef onto plates.

8. Fry the eggs sunny side up and put one on top of each piece of corned beef and serve.

28: Fried Egg Sandwich

A simple but delicious egg sandwich to nurse you back to health.

(Preparation time: 5 minutes/Serves: 1 serving)

Ingredients

- 2 slices of bread
- Butter
- 2 eggs
- Vegetable oil
- Ketchup

Directions

1. Heat the oil in a small frying pan over medium heat.

2. Butter both slices of bread.

3. Crack the eggs into the frying pan and cook on both sides until firm.

4. Put the eggs onto one slice of bread; squeeze some ketchup over the top.

5. Sandwich with the other slice and eat.

29: Hair on a Dog

This drink is an immediate pick me up.

(Preparation time: 5 minutes/Serves: 1 serving)

Ingredients

- 6 ounces of bulldog gin
- ½ an ounce of fresh lemon juice
- 3 splashes of Tabasco hot sauce
- 1 slice of chili pepper
- Ice

Directions

1. Pour the gin and the Tabasco sauce into a cocktail shaker filled with ice.

2. Shake vigorously.

3. Pour into a tall glass.

4. Put the chili pepper on top and drink.

30: Mexican Michelada

You've definitely won the battle with this drink.

(Preparation time: 5 minutes/Serves: 1 serving)

Ingredients

- 1 Mexican larger beer
- Clamato juice
- 3 dashes of hot sauce
- 2 dashes of Worcestershire sauce
- 2 dashes of soy sauce
- The juice of one lime

- Tajin seasoning

Directions

1. Sprinkle 1 teaspoon of Tajin onto a plate.

2. Rub the lime along the rim of the lime.

3. Turn the glass over and put the rim into the Tajin.

4. Fill 1/3 of the glass with the clamato juice.

5. Add the hot sauce.

6. Add the lime juice.

7. Add the Worcestershire sauce.

8. Add the soy sauce.

9. Pour the excess Tajin in the glass.

10. Fill the remainder of the glass with the Mexican larger.

11. Stir to combine.

12. Garnish with lime and drink.

Conclusion

Thank you once again for purchasing my book! We all like a drink but hate a hangover.......Typical! Every one of us is built differently, there are going to be some recipes that work for you and some that don't. Depending on how often you get hammered, experiment with them all and see which one works for you the best.

In the meantime, pop a couple of aspirins and go to bed! I wish you all the best in finding a hangover cure that works for you.

Author's Afterthoughts

Thanks ever so much to each of my cherished readers for investing the time to read this book!

I know you could have picked from many other books but you chose this one. So a big thanks for downloading this book and reading all the way to the end.

If you enjoyed this book or received value from it, I'd like to ask you for a favor. Please take a few minutes to post an honest and heartfelt review on Amazon.com. Your support does make a difference and helps to benefit other people.

Thanks!

Daniel Humphreys

About the Author

Daniel Humphreys

Many people will ask me if I am German or Norman, and my answer is that I am 100% unique! Joking aside, I owe my cooking influence mainly to my mother who was British! I can certainly make a mean Sheppard's pie, but when it comes to preparing Bratwurst sausages and drinking beer with friends, I am also all in!

I am taking you on this culinary journey with me and hope you can appreciate my diversified background. In my 15 years career as a chef, I never had a dish returned to me by one of clients, so that should say something about me! Actually, I will take that back. My worst critic is my four years old son, who refuses to taste anything that is green color. That shall pass, I am sure.

My hope is to help my children discover the joy of cooking and sharing their creations with their loved ones, like I did all my life. When you develop a passion for cooking and my suspicious is that you have one as well, it usually sticks for life. The best advice I can give anyone as a professional chef is invest. Invest your time, your heart in each meal you are creating. Invest also a little money in good cooking hardware and quality ingredients. But most of all enjoy every meal you prepare with YOUR friends and family!

Manufactured by Amazon.ca
Bolton, ON

23045882R00042